Say it with me!

words

that are

fun to say

volume 1

by Carol Perrine

artwork by Aja Dorsey & Mike Dorsey

2nd Edition

Easy Street Publishing
Gainesville, Florida

This book is not intended to replace dictionaries or grammar books.

Illustrations, artwork and graphic design by
Aja Dorsey and Mike Dorsey

Printed in the United States of America

First Printing, February, 2011   10 9 8 7 6 5 4

ISBN: 978-0-9832259-2-8

Library of Congress Control Number: 2011929829

Easy Street Publishing
2055 NE 9th St
Gainesville, FL 32609
www.EasySreetPublishing.com
Email: EasyStreetPublishing.@protonmail.com

Orders by U.S. trade bookstores and wholesalers, contact the publisher.

This book is dedicated to
my mother and father

Edith Octavia Perrine &
Robert Eugene Perrine (1925-1992)

&

my daughters,

Rose & Aja

Acknowledgements

My deepest gratitude and appreciation to my Mom, for all her help on so many levels including all her prayers for my success; to my wise, clever and creative daughters, Rose and Aja, who contributed not only great words, but also support, advice and encouragement; to Brad Tucker, who is kind and generous—his support has been invaluable; to Ruth Higgins, my friend and very patient life coach whose keen insight and excellent skills let me find my success; to Miranda Smith, an amazing editor, for allowing me to break almost all the rules of grammar, just this once; for their long hours and inventive illustrations, to artists and graphic designers Aja Dorsey and Mike Dorsey; to Danny Murawsky, for his sincere enthusiasm, web design, and tech support; to Nicole Pulcini Mason, for her great marketing advice, sense of style, and always being ready to help me when I need it the most.

Thank you to all my family and friends who have improved my life by laughing with me!

How to use this book

This book is for all ages and is designed to spark curiosity and enthusiasm for learning new and different words while having fun. If you see a word you don't know, find a dictionary and look it up.

FOR FUN: Read the word the way you think it is pronounced. Then, use the Pronunciation Key to sound it out. Notice the **bold** syllable for emphasis. Say the word a few times to get used to the way it is pronounced. If you are reading this book with someone, say it together out loud.

Each word has its part of speech abbreviated at the beginning of the definition. Use the Part of Speech Key for an explanation of how the word functions in the English language.

Read the definition and the sentence in which the word is used. **Write down words you don't know and look them up in a dictionary.**

Then, YOU create a sentence using the word that is fun to say!

*Words with an asterisk are SAT words. A more complete list can be found in
Say it with me! SAT words to know from Easy Street Publishing.

Note: It is infinitely more fun if you enunciate and emphasize the **bold** syllable when you say the words, and those are very good habits to cultivate anyway.

Part of Speech Key

n. noun – person, place, animal, thing, state or quality

Wow! Look at the amazingly intricate **artwork**.

v. verb – a word that describes performance of an action or existence of a state of being or condition

Wow! **Look** at the amazingly intricate artwork.

adj. adjective – used to describe a noun or pronoun and usually is placed just before the word it qualifies

Wow! Look at the amazingly **intricate** artwork.

adv. adverb – modifies a verb, adjective, another adverb or clause and answers the questions: To what degree? How? Where? When?

Wow! Look at the **amazingly** intricate artwork.

interjection – a brief exclamation used to express emotion and usually used in isolation

Wow! Look at the amazingly intricate artwork.

aardvark
ahrd-vahrk

n. A large nocturnal mammal with strong claws, long ears and a very long tongue that feeds on ants and termites and lives in Central and South Africa

Aarrr...the ship of pirate **aardvarks** sails the open sea!

abacus
ab-uh-kuhs

n. A device used for calculating that consists of a frame with rows of sliding beads; in architecture, a slab forming the top of a column

You can count on two meanings of **abacus.**

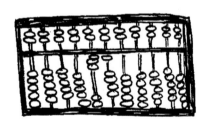

abalone
ab-uh-**loh**-nee

n. A sea-living creature having a bowl-like shell with a row of respiratory holes. The flesh is used for food and the shell is used for ornament and as a source of mother-of-pearl

Now, that sounds like a bunch of **abalone**,
but it's true!

abolishable
ah-**bah**-lish-uh-buhl

adj. Something that can be done away with completely; annulled; put an end to

Can you imagine if cruelty was **abolishable**?

abominable

uh-**bom**-uh-nuh-buhl

adj. Something that is repugnantly hateful, detestable or loathsome; disagreeable or very unpleasant

The **abominable** snowman that lived long ago popped balloons at parties and stole birthday cakes.

accelerometer
ak-sel-uh-**rom**-i-ter

n. An instrument for measuring acceleration of air-craft or guided missiles and also used for detecting and measuring vibrations

How fast can you say this word? You would know if you had an **accelerometer** built into your mouth.

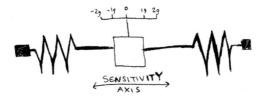

ambiguous*

am-**big**-yoo-uhs

adj. When something is not clear, has several possible meanings or is open to individual interpretation

Do you get my meaning or is it **ambiguous**?

*SAT Word

anonymity
an-uh-**nim**-i-tee

n. The quality or state of being unknown or unacknowledged

Superstars forget that those big sunglasses only pro-
tect their eyes and not their **anonymity.**

antecedent

an-tuh-**seed**-nt

n. In grammar, something that precedes a circumstance, event or object in a sentence. It is a word or phrase that is replaced by a pronoun or other substitute later in the same or another sentence.

Example: Edith lost a mitten and then she found it.
Edith is the **antecedent** of *she*
and *mitten* is the **antecedent** of *it*.

Got it? Say it anyway!

antithesis*
an-**tith**-uh-sis

n. The exact opposite or contrast

To dismiss a kiss is the **antithesis** of to acquiesce.

*SAT word

apiary
ay-pee-air-ee

n. A place where bees and beehives are kept and raised for honey

The ape created beautiful drapery
for the busy **apiary**.

arachnid
uh-**rak**-nid

n. This type of animal is what we usually call a spider, but it includes scorpions, mites, ticks and daddy longlegs. They have two parts to their bodies and eight legs, but no antennae or wings.

Arachnids are rascals but they need love, too. Anybody want four hugs?

baboon
ba-**boon**

n. A large terrestrial monkey from Arabia and Africa with a doglike muzzle, razor-sharp teeth, large cheek pouches and a short tail; slang for a person who is rude, ridiculous and usually of low intelligence

That big **baboon** is being rude!

babushka
buh-**boosh**-kuh

n. In Russia, the name of a scarf or hood with its strings, ends or two of the corners tied together under the chin; grandmothers were called this because they typically wore this type of scarf or hood.

Advice from a **babushka**: Don't you know it's freezing out there? Wear your **babushka**!

balaclava
bal-uh-**klah**-vuh

n. A close-fitting, knitted cap, worn especially by mountain climbers, soldiers and skiers, that covers the head, neck and tops of the shoulders

If it is *really* cold outside and your babushka just isn't enough, wear your **balaclava!**

begonia

bih-**gohn**-yuh

n. Any plant belonging to the Begonia genus, which is widely cultivated in warm tropical regions for their ornamental, succulent leaves and flowers that appear waxy

You are never alone if you've ever grown a **begonia**.

billabong
bil-uh-baung

n. Australian word meaning a branch of a river flowing away from the main stream but leading to no other body of water; a blind or dead-end channel; a dried up watercourse that holds water only in the rainy season

As you row along on a **billabong**
it's good to sing a cheery song.

bulbous
buhl-buhs

adj. Anything swollen, bulging or shaped like a bulb; growing from a bulb

There was little room left on the bus for us because everyone seemed a little **bulbous.**

bungalow
buhng-guh-loh

n. A small, single-story house or cottage with a thatched or tiled roof and a wide veranda or porch originally designed to provide affordable housing for the working class and now associated with romantic trysts in tropical locations

Stand on the veranda of your **bungalow**;
enjoy the view and the breezes that blow.

cacophony*
kuh-**kof**-uh-nee

n. A meaningless mixture of sounds that are often discordant, or not in harmony, much like city traffic at rush hour; in music, discords are used as emphasis to denote a relationship that is harsh, bad or evil

Your drums are creating a catastrophic **cacophony** and I'm trying to sleep!

*SAT Word

caladium
kuh-**lay**-dee-uhm

n. A variety of American plants widely cultivated for their ornamental leaves with various variegated patterns in white, green, pink or red

In southern regions, they adorn the landscape because people plant **caladium** after **caladium** after **caladium.**

Tweedledee and Tweedledum love to plant a
caladium.

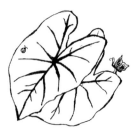

calendula
kuh-**len**-juh-luh

n. A plant with showy flowers of orange and yellow, also called pot marigold, has been used medicinally as a
diaphoretic to produce sweat and as a seasoning

The odiferous **calendulas** are blooming.
Come say "hello, **calendula**!"

candelabra

kan-dl-**ah**-bruh

n. Plural for candelabrum which is a candle holder
that has branches and each branch holds a candle

How many candles can those **candelabra** hold?

cantankerous
kan-**tang**-ker-uhs

adj. A person who is hard to get along with,
disagreeable and opposes anything suggested
(yes, anything)

The **cantankerous**, argumentative person disagreed
with everything. Yes, everything.

catacomb
kat-uh-kohm

n. An underground tunnel full of twists and turns and used as a cemetery with rooms cut out of the walls for coffins and tombs; the Catacombs, underground burial chambers of the early Christians near Rome, Italy

Hey, give that **cat a comb**! Although, a compass would be more practical in a **catacomb.**

cephalopod
sef-uh-luh-pod

n. Any of various marine mollusks such as the octopus, squid or cuttlefish having a large head, large eyes, prehensile sucker-bearing tentacles, and, in most species, an ink sac containing a dark fluid used for protection or defense

The card dealing **cephalopod** had an advantage even if he looked a bit odd.

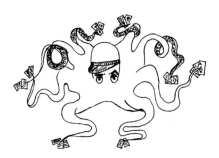

chasm
kaz-uhm

n. A deep, steep-sided opening in the earth's surface; also called an abyss or gorge

George went to the gorge and his heart gave a spasm; he thought, "This is a **chasm**."

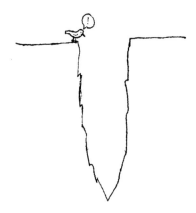

chrysanthemum

kri-**san**-thuh-muhm

n. A variety of plants with flowers of diverse colors and sizes, some with single ray petals and others with many layers of petals

His nerves went numb as he handed her a single **chrysanthemum.**

collegiality
kuh-lee-jee-**al**-i-tee

n. A number of colleagues who have shared authority and cooperative interaction; anything relating to a college

In an excellent show of **collegiality**, the bylaws were passed unanimously.

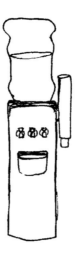

corollary
kawr-uh-lair-ee

n. An additional proposition that can be inferred or is an obvious deduction; a natural consequence or result from a proven proposition; an easily drawn conclusion

A long and healthy life is a **corollary**
of good habits and wise choices.

croak
krohk

v. To speak with a low harsh raspy voice; to be pessimistic or grumble about trouble or evil; slang meaning to die

"There's a curmudgeonly phantasm in that concertina," I heard the old man **croak** as I nervously set it back on the settee.

cruciferous
kroo-**sif**-er-uhs

adj. In botany, a family of plants having a corolla of four petals arranged to resemble a cross, including broccoli, collards and wasabi, to name a few; a person who carries a cross

Do not say **cruciferous** with your mouth full of wasabi.

crumple
kruhm-puhl

v. To press or crush, crinkle, rumple or wrinkle into a compact mass

Do not **crumple**, fold, spindle or mutilate!

deciduous
dih-**sij**-oo-uhs

adj. Shedding leaves annually at a particular stage of growth or season with a dormant period in certain trees and shrubs; transitory or not permanent as in leaves, teeth or horns

Pick up a rake and stop the fuss because *all* the trees are **deciduous**. What, not one evergreen?

dilapidated
dih-**lap**-i-day-tid

adj. A state of having fallen into decay or partial ruin from neglect, age or wear and tear

I bought a house and now I'm aggravated!
I didn't realize it was so **dilapidated**.

discombobulated

dis-kuhm-**bob**-yuh-lay-did

v. The past tense of discombobulate which means to throw into a state of confusion

We watched and corroborated as the ill-equipped politician **discombobulated** the reporters.

doodle
dood-l

v. To scribble or draw aimlessly during idle time, sometimes thought a foolish activity; to dawdle

n. A shape, picture or design made by aimless idle scribbling

I feuded with the rude dude over my **doodles** of snooty poodles eating noodles.

ecclesiastical
ih-**klee**-zee-as-ti-kuhl

adj. Anything that is churchly; pertaining to or of the church or clergy; not secular

The Sunday service is **ecclesiastical**
and even a little theatrical.

eclectic*
ih-**klek**-tik

adj. Diversity, as in a wide array of selection from various systems, doctrines or sources that seem to be the best

They elected to have an **eclectic** home with items that were sometimes electric.

*SAT Word

epiphany*
ih-**pif**-uh-nee

n. An insightful, intuitive perception into the essential meaning or reality of something, occurring suddenly and usually initiated by some simple, commonplace experience; an appearance, especially of a deity

"Eureka!" shouted Beethoven. "I've had an **epiphany** and now I can finish writing my symphony!"

*SAT word

eucalyptus

yoo-kuh-**lip**-tuhs

n. A tree indigenous to Australia cultivated for its timber, ornamental wood, and medicinal oils in its leaves

Eucalyptus leaves, medicinally, helps us breathe freely and easily.

euphonium
yoo-**foh**-nee-uhm

n. A brass musical instrument similar to the baritone tuba but somewhat smaller, with four valves; the ten-or of the tuba family with a mellower tone

Phone your friends for fun and ask if they play the
euphonium!

expeditious

ek-spi-**dish**-uhs

adj. A quality of promptness or quickness; done with speed and efficiency

The dinner was **expeditious** and delicious.

Bon Appétit!

explicable

ek-**splik**-uh-buhl

adj. When something is capable of being explained

The reason the Leaning Tower leans is entirely
explicable.

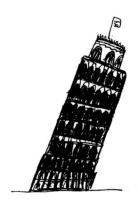

extemporaneous

ek-stem-puh-**ray**-nee-uhs

adj. Anything impromptu or done without advance preparation such as a performance or speech; something made especially for the occasion, like a shelter

It was obvious by the costumes that the performance was **extemporaneous** and even slightly heinous.

extravaganza
ek-strav-uh-**gan**-zuh

n. A production of a musical comedy or comic opera loose in structure and a frivolous theme with elaborate costumes and staging; any opulent, fanciful, lavish or showy event, literary or not

The elaborate gala was an exquisite **extravaganza.**

facetious

fuh-**see**-shuhs

adj. An attitude of levity that is not meant to be taken literally or seriously, as in a remark that is amusing or humorous and concerned with something frivolous, especially at inappropriate times

The **facetious** professor upset the supercilious students.

fastidious*
fa-**stid**-ee-uhs

adj. Excessively particular about details, hard to please, easily disgusted or very critical and demanding; requiring painstaking care

My **fastidious** sister is not invited back to the congeniality club.

*SAT Word

feeble
fee-buhl

adj. Physically weak, frail from age or sickness; intellectually or morally weak and indecisive or easily I nfluenced; lacking in force, strength or effectiveness, as in inadequate or unconvincing

He was so **feeble** he couldn't muster a fight even with a little boll weevil.

fiduciary
fi-**doo**-shee-air-ee

adj. An understanding of, or an obligation based on, the nature of trust and confidence, as in public affairs

My responsibility is **fiduciary** because, of course, it is considered customary.

filibuster
fil-uh-buhs-ter

n. This is a tactic used to delay legislative action, usually by extending and prolonging speeches by those who wish to obstruct the legislative process.

A person talks non-stop and fills up the time in a **filibuster**. If someone talks until the time runs out, no one can vote on the bill that they are talking about.

fjord
fyohrd

n. A Norwegian word meaning a long, narrow arm of the sea bordered by steep cliffs and usually formed by glacial erosion

Have you ever been to a **fjord**?
It is also spelled **fiord**.

TRY to say it without laughing.
TRY to say it while laughing.

flabbergasted
flab-er-gast-tid

adj. Amazed, bewildered, astounded or overcome with astonishment or surprise

Far from the farm, the **flabbergasted** family fled the big city.

fortuitous
fawr-**too**-i-tuhs

adj. A lucky or fortunate happening produced as if by chance or accident

Note: Fortuitous used to mean "happening by chance" and developed into "happening by lucky chance" and then became "lucky or fortunate." This probably occurred due to the similarity between the words fortuitous and fortunate.

How **fortuitous** for just the two of us to meet on the street.

gargantuan

gahr-**gan**-choo-uhn

adj. Huge; gigantic; colossal; enormous

Your **gargantuan** chrysanthemum
is very cumbersome!

gazebo

guh-**zee**-boh or guh-**zay**-boh

n. An open pavilion or summerhouse, sometimes with screen or latticework walls, built on a site that has an attractive view

You know where to go to watch your garden grow if you own your own **gazebo**.

gesundheit

guh-**zoont**-hahyt

interjection. A German word that literally means 'health', used as an expression to wish a person good health who has just sneezed

Did you "achoo?" **Gesundheit**!

gourd
gohrd

n. A plant that bears a fruit with a hard shell that when dried is used for bowls, bottles, dippers, flasks and ornaments

On your next trip to a fjord, take the versatile **gourd** on board.

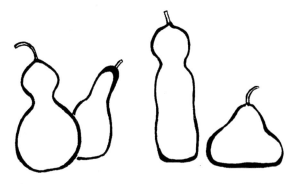

hematoma

hee-muh-**toh**-muh

n. A localized swelling filled with clotted or partially clotted blood resulting from a break in a blood vessel

Don't fall in Manitoba and develop a **hematoma**.

hippopotamus
hip-uh-**pot**-uh-muhs

n. A large herbivorous mammal having a thick hairless body, short legs, a large head and muzzle found in and near the rivers and lakes of Africa; named from a Greek word meaning "water horse" because they are able to remain under water for a considerable time

The **hippopotamus** sat upon us and we sunk to the bottom of the billabong.

hodgepodge
hoj-poj

n. A jumbled mixture of ingredients; a thick stew or soup made from meat and/or vegetables

Hodgepodge entrees include gazpacho and goulash.

hydrangea
hahy-**drayn**-juh

n. Several species of this shrub are cultivated for their large, beautiful and showy flowers of either white, pink or blue clusters. The dried roots have been used as a diuretic.

The voracious orangutan ate the
hydrangea arrangement.

hyperbole*
hahy-**per**-buh-lee

n. An obvious exaggeration made for effect and not meant to be taken literally, such as, "That man is as strong as an ox!" or, "That woman has a neck like a giraffe!"

It may offend your austere sensibilities when you hear a comedic **hyperbole**.

*SAT Word

hypnogogic
hip-nuh-**gog**-ik

adj. Being profoundly drowsy; the state of mind just before falling sound asleep

You are getting **hypnogogic**... you are getting *very* **hypnogogic**...

hypotenuse
hahy-**pot**-n-oos

n. The side of a right triangle that is opposite the right
angle

A playground is a lot more fun
when you make use of a **hypotenuse**.

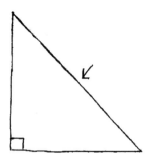

ichthyology
ik-thee-**ah**-luh-jee

n. A branch of zoology that deals with fishes. All the fishes. Lots and lots of fishes.

Under the sea goes the study of **ichthyology**.

iconography
ahy-kuh-**nog**-ruf-ee

n. The conventional symbolic representation of images used, such as drawing a cornucopia to represent the autumn harvest

Ecclesiastical **iconography** is the essence of Byzantine art.

imbue
im-**byoo**

v. To inspire or instill opinions, ideas, feelings or principles; rarely, to soak with moisture or dye

Look to someone you admire to **imbue**, renew or construe the best qualities in you.

indubitably
in-**doo**-bi-tuh-blee

adv. Without or beyond doubt; evidently; certainly; unquestionably

These ice cream cones are indubitably the most fabulous above and below the sea.

inoculate
ih-**nok**-yuh-layt

v. To introduce into a person, plant or animal a disease or substance to produce antibodies; to introduce microorganisms into a medium suited for their growth; to inspire a person, as with feelings, ideas or opinions

Inoculate your shiitake log and mushrooms will grow.

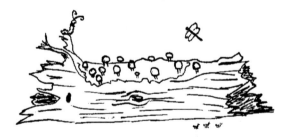

isosceles

ahy-**sos**-uh-leez

adj. In geometry, a triangle with two equal sides and angles

With veritable ease I drew an **isosceles**.

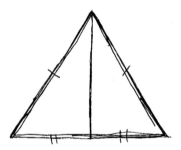

italicize

ahy-**tal**-uh-sahyz or ih-**tal**-uh-sahyz

v. To use italics, a style of print type designated by letters that usually slope slightly to the right and are used for emphasis or to separate information; to underscore with a single line to indicate italics

If you want to emphasize, go ahead and ***italicize***.

Jupiter
joo-pi-ter

n. The fifth planet from the sun and the largest planet in the solar system; also known as Jove, the supreme deity of the ancient Romans who was the god of weather and the heavens

Holy jumpin' **Jupiter**, that's a supremely big planet!

joust
jowst

n. A type of combat fought in a highly formalized manner, as part of a tournament, where two knights on horseback attempt to knock each other off their horses with blunted lances

v. to engage in such combat

> How many times have you been told,
> "Do not **joust** in the house!"

kapok
kay-pok

n. A silky fiber obtained from the fruit of the silk-cotton tree of the East Indies, Africa and tropical America: used for insulation and as padding in pillows, mattresses, and life preservers

This means that **kapok** is truly a life saver.

kazoo
kuh-**zoo**

n. A toy musical instrument with a membrane that produces a buzzing sound when a player hums or sings into the mouthpiece

He played his **kazoo**-zoo-zoo all the way to Kalamazoo-zoo-zoo. The temptation was there to drop him off at the zoo-zoo-zoo!

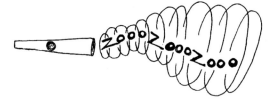

lackadaisical

lak-uh-**day**-zi-kuhl

adj. Lacking determination, interest, vitality or an active force of healthy, mental or physical energy; having sloth-like qualities, as in, being listless, lethargic or lazy.

When Daisy broke up with Ben
he became **lackadaisical**.

linoleum

li-**noh**-lee-uhm

n. A hard, washable floor covering formed by coating canvas or burlap with a combination of linseed oil, powdered cork and rosin with pigments to create the desired patterns and colors

Linoleum on your floors may last most of a millennium.

loblolly
lahb-lah-lee

n. A long-leaf pine tree with thick, bright red-brown bark and long needle-like leaves that grows in the swampy, sandy soils in the southern part of the United States; a mudhole or mire; a nautilus term for a thick gruel

I felt all wobbly as I lobbed along in the midst of the **loblolly**.

ludicrous
loo-di-kruhs

adj. Something that is absurd; provoking or deserving derision due to the ridiculous or laughable nature of a situation; an obvious absurdity or incongruity

The amphibious platypus looks quite **ludicrous**.

lugubrious
loo-**goo**-bree-uhs

adj. A mournful, dismal or gloomy state of being, especially to an exaggerated degree; an unrelieved manner

The **lugubrious** opossums never wanted to stop playing dead.

lumbago
luhm-**bay**-goh

n. In the study of disease, this is recurring or chronic pain in the lower, lumbar region of the back

Let's rest and eat a bagel
while you nurse your **lumbago**.

marsupial
mahr-**soo**-pee-uhl

n. Non-placental mammals, including wombats, bandicoots, kangaroos and opossums, the female of which has a pouch or fold of skin where the young are born, feed and continue to grow, living mostly in Australia, South and Central America

All the **marsupial** friends danced the rumba, the mambo and the meringue. Hooray!

memento
muh-**men**-toh

n. An object such as a keepsake or souvenir that serves to remind one of a person or past event. A very early meaning was "something that serves to warn."

Do you keep a sentimental **memento**
like an olive keeps a pimento?

minuscule
min-uh-skyool

adj. Something very small; in writing, referring to letters that are lower case

A very small school is a **miniscule** school.

monofilament
mon-uh-**fil**-uh-muhnt

n. Material used for typical fishing line that is made from a single, large, untwisted synthetic fiber such as nylon

You can mend a home with multi-purpose **monofilament** and duct tape.

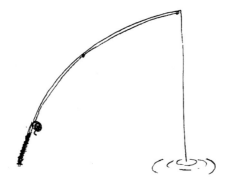

mononucleosis
mah-noh-noo-klee-**oh**-sis

n. An infectious, yet self-limiting, viral disease with
acute symptoms that include fever, general exhaustion
and swelling of the lymph nodes

Now you know to just say no to **mononucleosis**.
It's fun to say and not fun to have.
There is nothing cute about the symptoms!

GETTIN' MILKSHAKES WITH YOUR
NEW SWEETIE...

UNSaFE   SaFER

OR JUST ORDER TWO SMALLS.
SaFEST!

mukluk
muhk-luhk

n. A soft boot worn by Eskimos, usually made of sealskin or reindeer skin and often lined with fur; a similar soft-soled boot worn for lounging

Merrily and heartily hike an arctic trail in your **mukluks**!

narcissism
nahr-suh-siz-uhm

n. A high degree of fascination and admiration with oneself to the point of excessive vanity and self-love

Narcissism loves itself so much, it gave itself all the 's' sounds it could find!

nefarious
ni-**fair**-ee-uhs

adj. Evil; extremely wicked; sinful; villainous

The abominable snowman is the hairiest of the
nefarious beasts.

octopus

ok-tuh-puhs

n. An animal with a soft, oval body and eight sucker-bearing, prehensile arms and, most of the time, living at the bottom of the sea; an expression for an organization that has far reaching control or influence, especially a harmful one

The **octopus,** squid and the cuttlefish went to a cephalopod party!

odiferous
oh-**dif**-er-uhs

adj. Having, yielding or diffusing an odor or fragrance;
a shortened version of the word, odoriferous

The smell from the garden is so delicious because the
blossoms are extraordinarily **odiferous**.

ogle
oh-guhl

v. To look or stare at in an amorous, flirtatious, or impertinent manner

The paparazzi loved to **ogle** the media mogul.

onomatopoeia
on-uh-ma-tuh-**pee**-uh

n. The formation or use of words such as zap, whack, buzz or murmur that imitate the sounds associated with the objects or actions to which they refer; used for rhetorical or poetic effect

Is crumple the lost **onomatopoeia**?
Just look and listen.

opulent
op-yuh-luhnt

adj. Describing abundance or wealth, as in plentiful or richly supplied

She reclined on a velvet chaise wearing her jewels and furs in her **opulent** well-appointed salon.

pagoda
puh-**goh**-duh

n. A tower that is pyramid-like and several stories high that typically has an upward curving roof for each story; originally, serving religious purposes as a temple, sacred building, or shrine in India and the Far East

Please remove all mukluks before entering the **pagoda.**

pantomime

pan-tuh-mahym

n. The art of conveying actions and emotions with gestures and bodily actions and no speech; entertainment in which the performers do the same to the accompaniment of music

One day, if you meet a mime, watch how he tells you,
in **pantomime,** that he is a friend of mine.

parallelogram
pair-uh-**lel**-uh-gram

n. In geometry, a four-sided figure having both pairs of opposite sides parallel and equal to each other such as a rectangle or diamond

Would you rather receive a telegram, candy-gram or **parallelogram**?

paramecium

pair-uh-**mee**-see-uhm

n. A freshwater, one-celled organism that is covered with cilia and has a long deep grove for taking in nutrients

Who wants to dress up like a **paramecium** for Halloween? What, no one?

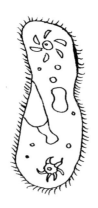

perfunctory
per-**fuhngk**-tuh-ree

adj. Lacking interest and merely performing a task without care or enthusiasm in an indifferent, dull or apathetic manner; hasty, routine or superficial

Put some fun in your **perfunctory** performance or the audience will skedaddle.

pernicious
per-**nish**-uhs

adj. Something or someone that causes grave harm or ruin; seemingly harmless but is actually hurtful; wicked; malicious; deadly

Be on the alert if something seems suspicious; it may be **pernicious.**

perpendicular

per-puhn-**dik**-yuh-ler

adj. This refers to being straight up and down, vertical or upright; in geometry, it is where a given line meets a surface at right angles

These particular **perpendicular** people were prone to falling over.

persnickety
per-**snik**-i-tee

adj. An informal word to describe the characteristic of being excessively precise and fussy; an exacting, over-particular attention to detail; being snobbish and requiring painstaking care

My ancient aunt was incredibly **persnickety**, but she left me a bundle.

petunia
pi-**toon**-yuh

n. A plant native to tropical America cultivated for its funnel-shaped white, blue, pink or deep reddish-purple flowers

Do you prefer a **petunia** or a begonia on the veranda?

phantasm
fan-taz-uhm

n. An appearance, real or imagined, of a supernatural person or thing that can be startling, surprising or terrifying, like a ghost. Boo!

In the depths of the chasm he thought he was being followed by a curious **phantasm**.

phenomenon
fi-**nohm**-uh-non

n. Something that is considered impressive or extraordinary; a person that is exceptional such as a prodigy; a fact that can be directly observed by the senses without using a hypothesis, as in nature

On many levels, a ten-pound guanabana is a **phenomenon.**

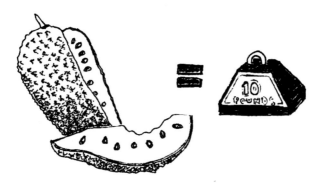

Piccadilly

pik-uh-dihl-ee

n. A major London street, running from Hyde Park Corner in the west to Piccadilly Circus in the east; named after a piccadill, a stiff collar with scalloped edges and broad lace or perforated borders that was manufactured in that area and popular in the 1600's

If you want to visit **Piccadilly** Street you must dress precisely perfect and neat.

pituitary
pi-**too**-i-tair-ee

n. An endocrine gland that is the size of a pea located at the base of the brain that secretes six hormones that regulate homeostasis

Mary was feeling contrary because of an upset in her **pituitary**.

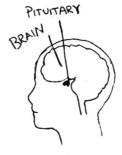

platypus
plat-i-puhs

n. A small aquatic, egg-laying, venomous mammal of Australia and Tasmania having otter-like webbed feet, a bill resembling that of a duck and a tail like a beaver

The peculiar **platypus** played the piccolo.

plethora*
pleth-er-uh

n. An overabundance or excess

Would you say twenty piñatas is a
plethora of piñatas?

*SAT Word

polypropylene
pol-ee-**proh**-puh-leen

n. Tough, flexible materials that are made by polymerizing propylene, used chiefly for molded parts, electrical insulation, packaging, bottles and fibers for wearing apparel

Simply put, a plastic polymer of propylene is a **polypropylene.**

Pythagorean

pi-thag-uh-**ree**-uhn

adj. Referring to Pythagoras, a Greek philosopher, mathematician, and religious reformer; also referring to his school or doctrines

How many times can you quickly say **Pythagorean** Theorem?

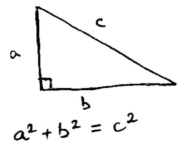

$$a^2 + b^2 = c^2$$

rabble-rouser
rab-uhl-row-zer

n. A person, especially a politician, who gains power by arousing the passions or prejudices of the public, usually for his or her own
interests

Are we imagining things or are **rabble-rousers** relatively regular these days?

rhododendron
roh-duh-**den**-druhn

n. A genus of over 1000 species that are usually the size of a shrub or small tree best known for showy flower displays with many clusters of large flowers; the national flower of Nepal, the state tree of Sikkim (a state in the Himalayas), and the state flower of both West Virginia and Washington State in the USA

The showy **rhododendron** grows on many roads, don't you suppose?

sagacity*
suh-**gas**-i-tee

n. The quality of being discerning; sound in judgment; keen mental acuteness

The **sagacity** of the crew was impressive as they maneuvered down the fjord.

*SAT word

sarcophagus
sahr-**kof**-uh-guhs

n. A stone or marble coffin or tomb, especially one bearing inscriptions or sculpture often displayed as a monument and usually made from limestone

One could go their whole life and not know what a **sarcophagus** is until the end.

Sasquatch
sas-kwahch

n. A very large, hairy, human-like creature, as folklore would have it, who leaves very big foot prints and inhabits the wilderness areas of the Pacific Northwest in the U.S. and Canada

Keep on the watch for **Sasquatch!**

sassafras
sas-uh-fras

n. An American tree of the laurel family having odd-shaped leaves and long clusters of greenish yellow flowers; the aromatic bark of its root is used medicinally and for flavoring beverages and confectionery

I'll take a **sassafras** soda, you silly sapsucker.

schefflera
shef-**lair**-uh

n. A variety of tropical trees or shrubs that belong to the ginseng family with glossy leaves that are widely cultivated as indoor plants because of their tolerance to low light conditions

Schefflera is one of the softest words you will find.
It floats off your tongue like a cloud
being carried by a breeze.

schism
skiz-uhm

n. The separation, division or disunion into opposing factions caused by a difference of opinion, breach or discord

It looks like there was a **schism**
down there in the chasm.

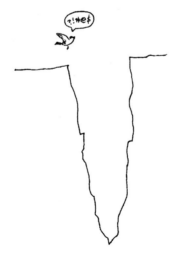

serendipity
sair-uhn-**dip**-i-tee

n. An aptitude for making lucky and fortunate discoveries by accident while looking for something else

Note: It comes from the Persian fairy tale "The Three Princes of Serendip," whose heroes, due to sagacity and accidents, made discoveries of things they were not in quest of.

What **serendipity** it is to find a fish in the mesh of your net that you didn't mean to get!

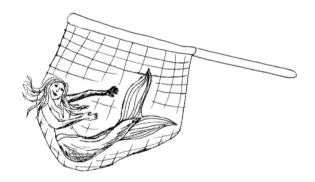

shenanigan
shuh-**nan**-i-guhn

n. An informal word that indicates mischief, trickery or prankishness

Sister Mary Edwin frowned upon any and all signs of a **shenanigan**.

simultaneous

sahy-muhl-**tay**-nee-uhs

adj. Anything that is happening, existing, or done at
the same time, as in concurrent

The strange and **simultaneous**
series of sounds created a cacophony.

skedaddle

ski-**dad**-l

v. A slang word meaning to betake one's self away as if in a panic or simply to flee; to leave or run away hurriedly

Shoo, fly, **skedaddle** and betake yourself to flight away from here!

snare

snair

n. A trap, as in getting caught up in something; a noose used to catch game; a string or wire used on the bottom of a drum

Avoid the **snare** of snazzy clothes purely for popularity for there is a high price to pay.

snazzy
snaz-ee

adj. An informal way of describing things, especially clothes, which are stylish, attractive and often flashy

Her nickname was Jazzy because her clothes were so **snazzy!**

soliloquy
suh-**lil**-uh-kwee

n. An act or instance of talking to oneself, oblivious to others, such as an actor speaking lines in a drama in which the character reveals thoughts to the audience but not to the other characters

The actor turned to the audience—as if secretly—and spoke a **soliloquy**.

solipsistic
sol-ip-**sis**-tik

adj. The theory that nothing can exist but the self and the self is the only object of real knowledge; egotistic self-absorption; preoccupation with one's desires and feelings

Everything out there is an illusion to those who are **solipsistic**.

specificity

spes-uh-**fis**-i-tee

n. The quality of being specific; explicit, definite or particular

The speaker made it perfectly clear that you could most certainly rely on her **specificity!**

spittoon
spi-**toon**

n. A large bowl used as a receptacle for spit, especially from chewing tobacco, widely used in the 19th and early 20th centuries, often made of metal and kept in a public place; also, known as a cuspidor

The saloon had a **spittoon** and a tinny-sounding piano that played its own tune.

spoof
spoof

n. Usually a light-hearted and good-humored hoax or prank; a light mocking imitation of someone or something

A surreptitious **spoof** of old becomes legend as it's retold.

supercilious

soo-per-**sil**-ee-uhs

adj. A person or a facial expression that displays a haughty, snobbish indifference or arrogant disdain

How silly it is to be **supercilious** when we are all just the same.

superfluous

soo-**per**-floo-uhs

adj. Being excessive or more than is required to the point of needless, unnecessary, or irrelevant

Super powers are sufficient, but super-duper powers might be **superfluous** powers!

surreptitious
ser-uhp-**tish**-uhs

adj. A secret, clandestine or unauthorized manner, as in to obtain, make, or do something by stealth; to act in that same stealthy or secret manner

The meeting had to be **surreptitious** and expeditious before their location was discovered.

syllabub
sil-uh-buhb

n. A mildly sweet dessert made of milk or cream with wine or cider and often made with eggs, nutmeg and cinnamon; a spiced drink often served hot made with rum, wine or port; referring to writing that is insubstantial and thought of as frothy in content

It is far more rewarding to make and eat
or drink than to write a **syllabub.**

symbiotic
sim-bee-**ah**-tic

adj. Any mutually beneficial or interdependent relationship between two persons, groups or even different species that live together

The relationship of the shark and remora is not just aquatic, it's **symbiotic**.

synchronicity
sing-kruh-**nis**-i-tee

n. The simultaneous or coincidental occurrence of events and especially psychic events that seem related but are not explained by conventional theories of cause and effect

It was **synchronicity** to be in that club at that time in that country.

taffeta
taf-i-tuh

n. A fancy and delicate fabric made of medium or light weight rayon, nylon, acetate or silk that is usually crisp and smooth with a luster or shine

I won't laugh at ya if you spill half of a carafe on your **taffeta**.

tissue
tish-yoo

n. A disposable towel or handkerchief made of thin absorbent paper consisting of one, two or more layers; a large number of cells, as part of an organism that has a similar structure and function such as nerve or connective tissue

Gesundheit! Would you like me to issue
a **tissue** to you?

toboggan
tuh-**bog**-uhn

n. A long and narrow flat sled without runners with the front curved up toward the back used for sliding over snow or ice

Do you think it is more fun to **toboggan** in Cheboygan or Ontonagon?

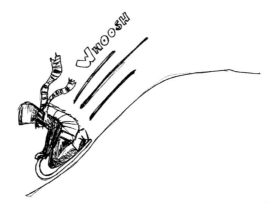

trattoria

trah-tuh-**ree**-uh

n. An informal café or restaurant that serves primarily Italian dishes, usually inexpensively

A **trattoria** is a welcome sight for any size appetite.

tsunami

tsoo-**nah**-mee

n. An unusually large and often destructive sea wave produced by an undersea volcanic eruption or sea-quake; a seismic sea wave

A **tsunami** can be a sizeable seismic wave!

tupelo
too-puh-loh

n. Any group of trees growing in moist places in the southern United States, especially the water gum or sour gum trees with light tough wood used for furniture, boxes, pulpwood and crates; the flowers produce wonderful honey with a light color and buttery flavor

The ants march in a row below while the bees buzz up above around the **tupelo**.

tutu
too-too

n. A short, full skirt, usually made of several projecting layers of stiffened sheer material, such as tarlatan or tulle, worn by ballerinas

A **tutu** made of tulle makes it fun to dance and twirl.

tympani
tim-puh-nee

n. The plural of tympano which is a kettle drum

The chimpanzee played the **tympani** rather gleefully,
don't you think?

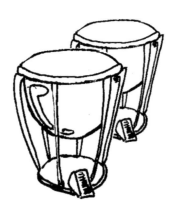

ubiquitous
yoo-**bik**-wi-tuhs

adj. What seems to exist everywhere, or in all places, at the same time; omnipresent; in a humorous or casual way, it can be applied to what seems to appear all over the place

Is there anything you would like, more or less, to become **ubiquitous**?

ukulele

yoo-kuh-**lay**-lee or oo-k*oo*-**lay**-lay

n. A four-stringed miniature guitar-like instrument, originally from Portugal, and then popular in the Hawaiian Islands. At first it was a nickname for a nimble player and later applied to the instrument itself.

Do you play the **ukulele?** How do *you* say **ukulele?**

vector

vek-ter

n. The direction or course followed by an airplane, missile and other similar aircraft, from one point to another within a given time

Check your **vector**, Victor! Find a director, Hector!

wallaby
wol-uh-bee

n. A type of small and medium-sized kangaroos native to Australia, some of which are no larger than rabbits; some species are endangered

Imagine what a **wallaby** would do in Walla Walla, Washington.

Yanomamo
yah-nuh-**mah**-moh

n. An indigenous people located in southern Venezuela and northern Brazil who live in the Amazon tropical rain forest

The **Yanomamo** build thatch bungalows where it never snows.

zanthoxylum

zan-tho-**zahy**-lum

n. A genus of approximately 250 species of deciduous and evergreen trees and shrubs in the rue or citrus family native to warm climates and often used for bonsai trees; historically, the bark was used to treat toothaches, rheumatism and colic

Take asylum in the land of the **zanthoxylum.**

zebra
zee-bruh

n. A member of the horse family having distinctive black stripes on a whitish background and native to Southern and Eastern Africa

The exuberant **zebra** celebrated by playing the kazoo and the xylophone simultaneously.

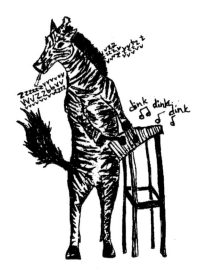

MORE FUN WITH WORDS

The Laughing Game

With a group of people—the more the merrier—write a fun word on a small piece of paper for each person and put the words in a hat or bowl. Then, each person draws a piece of paper and takes a turn saying the word loudly so everyone can hear it.

Then EVERYONE says the word loudly together and laughs a lot.

Card Game

Make 25 game cards with a word on one side and its part of speech and definition on the other side. Lay them down definition side down in rows of 5. Each turn consists of a player choosing a word card. If the player can recite the definition, the player keeps the card and gets a point. If not, the player reads the card aloud and puts it back in its place. It is then the next player's turn. A card may not be picked twice in a row. A bonus point is earned for knowing the part of speech. Continue turns until all cards have been picked up.

The one who laughs the most wins!

Carol Perrine, originally from Flint, MI, now lives and laughs in Gainesville, FL. Loving, laughing and learning are her favorite things to do and she comes from a long line of loving and laughing learners.

Her passion is to inspire others to introduce the joy of learning in a fun way to any age person, but especially to young children when brain development is in a critical period, because life can be more fun when you are smart.

Aja Dorsey lives and draws in Gainesville, FL. Likes: wide-spectrum cleverness, movement and lucky saves. Dislikes: logical fallacies and flat tires.

Mike Dorsey was born in Gainesville, FL. He has been writing songs for most of his life and his group is called *Princess Parade*.

Look for more books by

Carol Perrine

in the

Say it with me! series

from

Easy Street Publishing

Say it with me! WORDS THAT ARE FUN TO SAY:
VOL. 2

Say it with me! PLACES THAT ARE FUN TO SAY

Say it with me! FOOD THAT IS FUN TO SAY

www.EasySreetPublishing.com
EasyStreetPublishing.@protonmail.com

Do you know a word that is fun to say?
What is your favorite word from this book?

WRITE TO US!

Easy Street Publishing
Attn: Fun Word Dept.
2055 NE 9th St
Gainesville, FL 32609

EMAIL US!

EasyStreetPublishing.@protonmail.com

Be sure to include your return contact information.

YOUR FUN WORDS & DRAWINGS

YOUR FUN WORDS & DRAWINGS